My Pain is
MY POWER

By: Tanisha Bankston

Book Completion Services Provided by:
TRU Statement Publications
www.trustatementpublications.com

Second Edition: July 2021
Printed in the United States of America
0 7 0 3 2 0 2 1
ISBN: 9798531401502

Contents

Introduction

My pain is my power because I endured so much pain as a child, starting from the age of five years old when I was taken away from my mother and separated from my brothers and sister. I continued to endure pain throughout my adulthood. I was like a caterpillar in a cocoon, waiting to hatch out of its shell into a butterfly. My inner voice was trapped until I found God and He allowed me to speak out.

I talk to you about how I was raped and was not believed, and how the rape, manipulation, childhood sexual abuse, and domestic violence kept happening. So, by me not being believed, I was sent into a shell that I didn't come out of. I was failed by the system and some of my family members.

I never thought I would become a mother at the tender age of 14 and 17. I was a teen mom of two children by my cousin's husband and a neighborhood man. I never thought I would experience domestic violence at the tender age of 14. I am most definitely a survivor. I had to protect myself because I was never protected by my family or the system.

I am just now coming out of my shell at the age of 32 years old. I am starting to heal and find myself. I pray my book helps others to open up and tell their story. Even when your voice trimmers or shakes, SPEAK UP AND SPEAK OUT! Our mind has been so traumatized. The mind and FEAR will tell you that you can't do it. I am here to tell you, "YES YOU CAN!"

My book is dedicated to my three children and to the victims and survivors of childhood sexual abuse, trauma, pain, domestic violence, molestation, and rape. I believe you. My favorite scripture is, "I can do all things through Christ Jesus who strengthens me," Philippians 4:13. I choose Faith over Fear.

My Pain is MY POWER

Taken from My Mother and Separated from My Siblings

I am a 32-year-old mother of three beautiful children. My oldest daughter's name is Iyonia Bankston, and she is 18 years old. My son's name is Rodriquez Bankston. He goes by the name of Malik, which is his middle name, and he is 15 years old. My third and last child is my baby girl, Khloe, and she is 3 years old. I am a Certified Pharmacy Technician and a Licensed Insurance Agent. I am the oldest of four children. My brothers, sister, and I were all taken away from our mom at a young age.

My mom had me when she was 16 years old. She was just a kid herself, trying to raise and take care of kids. She had my eldest brother when she was 17 years old, had my sister when she was 18 years old, and had my baby brother when she was 19 years old. I felt like after talking to my mom and hearing her side of the story, she tried her best at raising four kids at a young age.

My mom neglected us as kids. She would always leave us home while she went out and chased behind men. My mom had some serious problems. She used to drink all the time. There were days we would see our mom getting beat by men. She would be fighting them back, but it traumatized me as a child, seeing the things that my mom went through with men. I remember when a man beat my mom with a hammer in front of me and blood was everywhere. They had gotten into an argument. I cried saying stop, and I was grabbing her leg.

One day my mom had punched her arm through a window at the house and broke the glass and put me through the window to unlock the front door. All I saw was the blood running from my mom's arm from her being cut on the broken glass. I have a scar on my back from me getting cut by the glass on the window when my mom put me through the window.

I failed kindergarten because my mom did not send me to school. I missed over 60 days. I remember my mom perming my hair and all of my hair fell out because she had been drinking and mixed the perm wrong. I had a lot of bald spots in my head from the chemicals taking my hair out.

There were a lot of days that my brothers, sister and I didn't have any food to eat. I remember us eating flour out of the cabinet because we were so hungry. We were so hungry that our stomach was hurting, and we were crying.

My mom would leave us home alone while she would be gone. She used to bathe us outside in a pink hospital pan with the fire burning. I am assuming she did that because our lights were off. I really don't remember any fun activities playing with my brothers and sister. All I remember is us being hungry, crying in the house for food, and being taken away by the welfare people.

I used to love being with my mom when I was little. She used to take me to Spain's and buy me candy. One day my mom, her guy friend, and I were walking down the street by the courthouse. My mom and the guy had gotten into an argument and the guy had started jumping on my mom and he hit her with a broom. My mom had pulled out a box cutter and started cutting the man all over. I saw blood everywhere. The man had put his hands up, trying to get my mom to stop cutting him. It was like she had snapped; I guess she was tired of taking beatings from men. My mom was bad about cutting people. She ended up going to prison for some years for cutting that man. The system is so messed up. The man had jumped on my mom and she defended herself. That was domestic violence!

My mom spent most of our childhood in prison. I remember one night my baby brother and I were at our aunt's house and a song came on by Faith Evans and Sean Combs aka Puff Daddy called, "I'll Be Missing You." We both started crying because we were missing our mom. She used to write us letters all the time, telling us how much she missed us. All we wanted was to be with our mom and for her to come home. I didn't know that my mom had been dealing with Mental Illness and had been raped herself until just recently. I had to have been 6 years old when DHS took me. My eldest brother's grandparents and his dad had gotten custody of him. My sister's aunt had gotten custody of her. My aunt ended up getting custody of me and my youngest brother.

I Lost My Inner Voice 2

I was once a happy child until I was raped at the age of 5 or 6 by a man who used to be at my grandmother's house. I used to love playing with my friends and my cousins. My grandmother and everyone had left her house and went to my great grandmother's house. My grandmother stayed across the railroad tracks from my great grandmother.

I didn't go because I was sleepy, so I stayed at the house and laid in the bed until I fell asleep. I remember the man not leaving the house. He stayed there too. I remember seeing him out of the corner of my eye. He was standing at the corner of the hallway. I had finally gone to sleep. I felt somebody on top of me. When I opened my eyes he was on top of me, spreading my legs open. He forced himself in me. I was trying to scream and cry, but he had his hand over my mouth so I couldn't scream.

I remember him like it was yesterday. I remember seeing that scar above his eye. There was a carousel lamp on the floor, and it had oil in it. I was trying to scream and was kicking, and he was still in me. I managed to get him off me by kicking him in his private part. I got up, and I ran across the railroad tracks crying to my mom. My mom asked me what was wrong with me and I told her that man had touched me down there.

At age 5 or 6 years old, I didn't understand or know what the word rape meant. But that man had raped me. My mom had called the ambulance. I was taken to the hospital by ambulance. I was placed on a table in a dark room. I remember seeing blood on the sheets. My mom said that the doctors and nurse wouldn't allow her to come in the room with me. My mom said I was taken to a special hospital. She said I had to relearn how to walk again due to the man messing my legs up.

I remember going to this place and looking out of a window with a gown on. I could see myself looking out of the window. It was like my soul had left my body. I went into a shell and never came out. I hid myself. I isolated myself within myself. I changed when I was raped.

The man who raped me was in his 30s. He was never locked up. My mom told me that she almost went to prison because they told her that she had neglected me. I don't understand why my mom would have gone to prison and not the man who raped me. My mom said she had let my grandmother and her sisters watch me that night. My mom told me that the police said they didn't have enough proof that the man had raped me. But I know he had done that to me. Why would a child make that up? To this day that man is still out on the street living his life, while I am trying to find myself and my life. He destroyed my childhood and my excitement.

My brain was even traumatized more due to being raped. I had already been traumatized from being taken away from my mom, separated from my siblings, and seeing my mom get beaten by men.

I had one cousin who passed away when she was 15 years old from AIDS. We did everything together. She was like a sister to me. I cried like a baby when I got the phone call that my cousin had died. Men used to have sex with my cousin all the time, and one of our cousins used to have sex with her a lot as well when we were young. Grown men were manipulating my cousin into having sex with them for money. She was gang raped by some guys in Greenwood, MS. The guys had left her for dead. My mom said that she and her husband had found her laying outside by their car.

I also used to play with my friends and other cousins. I had another favorite cousin who I used to love playing with a lot. We did everything together. I used to laugh, play, and sing in the shower and I stopped doing that when that man stole my childhood, and other grown men, as well.

It hurt the most because no one believed me! One day, I had seen the man who raped me at Pizza Hut and I said to him, "You're the man who raped me!"

And he said, "I didn't do anything to you. I don't know who told you that, but I didn't touch you."

I know what he did to me. I don't like seeing that man. I feel like he should be punished for what he did to me. He's out walking freely. There is no telling who else he is doing that to or has done it to.

As I got older, I started asking my mom questions about why that man didn't get locked up for raping me. My mom said that he said he didn't do anything to me. My mom said when my uncle had gotten out of training school, he had jumped on the man for what he had done to me.

I never received therapy or counseling after I left the hospital. I went through a lot to go through as a child. I had shut down from everybody. People used to say that I was shy. I had a reason for being shy. In school, I was easily distracted.

My childhood had been stolen from me. I was not only raped, but I wasn't believed. The system failed me. They didn't protect me. It was like they believed the man over me. I still hurt 'til this very day. Growing up, I didn't know how to stand up for myself. I was always bullied.

Manipulated 3
To Have Sex At 10 Years Old

I thought I would have been safer with my aunt, but it seems like I was in a worser condition. The rape and sexual abuse kept happening. One of my aunt boyfriends had started having sex with me. He was in his 30s. He would give me money, like $1 dollar bills and penny wrappers with pennies or dimes in it and take me to what was called the *dog pound,* back in the days, and have sex with me.

After he would have sex with me, he would tell me to go home and take a bath and not to tell anyone. So, I didn't. I felt like no one would believe me anyway because I wasn't believed when I was 5 or 6 years old. Once again, I was failed by my family and the system.

My aunt's boyfriend would come to my aunt's

house and watch me. He would wink his eye at me. When I would leave my aunt's house, he would leave too and tell me to meet him on Church St. between two houses that had a plum tree. Deep down on the inside of me, I didn't want to meet him. I didn't know how to say "No," so I went on. He would tell me how beautiful I was and told me not to tell anyone what he had been doing to me. I was afraid to tell anyone. So, I didn't.

I wanted to say something so badly, but I was afraid. I had already lost my inner voice from the first man raping me and not being believed. And if I did tell it, would I be believed this time?

Like I said earlier, people had always labeled me as being shy growing up. It was a reason I was being shy; I was being touched and raped by grown men who knew better, yet they manipulated an innocent child. They stole my childhood. My family never knew about what my aunt's boyfriend/baby daddy had been doing to me. I just recently spoke about all the bad things that happened to me, as a child, on July 3, 2020. I just recently told my aunt, in January 2021, who has kids by the man, what he had done to me.

One of the men's daughter, who is my cousin, said some very hateful things about me when I spoke on a radio talk show. She didn't know that her dad was one of the men who had taken advantage of a child and raped and manipulated me. I don't think she would have believed me or cared, anyway.

I was never protected by my family. I was never taught or told to speak up and tell it if anyone tries to touch you *down there* and to know that you have the right to say "No." I was so traumatized by all that was going on with me and happening to me. All from neighborhood men. My body had been tossed around like I was nothing.

MY PAIN IS MY POWER

Manipulated
To Have Sex At 11 Years Old

4

Every man who touched me was a grown man from the neighborhood. I used to go to the neighborhood candy store to buy candy and snacks with the money my aunt's boyfriend was giving me. The neighborhood grandson had started watching me. He started writing me letters and giving them to me. He used to tell me how pretty I was. As I continued to go to the store, he started giving me free candy and whatever I wanted. One day, he asked me if I wanted to be his girlfriend. I didn't know what to say, or I didn't know how to say no. He had been telling people that I was his girlfriend. He had started calling me "Black Barbie."

I had already been manipulated by other grown men. One morning, I went to go buy some candy, and he was the one who answered the door. He told me to get whatever I wanted. Then he told me to come to the back room. His grandfather asked him who was that, and he said, "Nobody." He took me into the room and closed the door. He had a letter that he had written to me and had a blanket laying on the floor like he had already planned what he did to me. He laid me on the floor and pulled out a red condom. He said it was going to be ok. He said it's not going to hurt and I'm not going to hurt you. That was the first time he had sex with me, and it wasn't the last time. I was 11 years old. He was in his 30s. I was scared and didn't know what to say. It hurt so badly; I was crying on the inside. He would put his long fingers inside of me and finger me.

As the sexual abuse kept happening, he would come to my aunt's house and knock on my window at night. I didn't have any blinds or sheet at the window. Why? I don't know. All I remember was seeing a black shadow, and it was him. He would have me to sneak out of the window at night. I have a scar on my back from me hurting myself on the bricks. He would get me to walk with him and meet him on the railroad tracks or at his grandparent's house.

Some nights were cold outside, and he would pick me up and put me in the empty containers and take off his black leather coat and lay it on the floor and tell me to lay down and would take my clothes off and have sex with me. After he was done having sex with me, he would walk me back to my aunt's house and pick me up and put me back in the window and I would lie down and go to sleep. I felt so sticky and nasty.

He would also get me to miss school to take me to the motel or to his friend's house to have sex with me. One morning, he had his friend and his friend girlfriend to take us to a motel. The school had called my aunt and told her that I wasn't at school. She must have called the police because the police had come to the motel where were at. He had gotten the motel in his friend's name. He did that just in case the police came looking for us. The man was just about to have sex with me, but the police had knocked on the door. He hid me in between the mattress and box spring. That's just how small and little I was. The police had looked under the bed and I wasn't there.

They were about to leave, but one police said, "Wait!" and he lifted up the mattress and I was laying there. The police told me to get up and come with him. They almost didn't see me.

The police had handcuffed the man who had taken me to the motel. I was taken to the hospital. A rape test had been done on me. I remember the nurse putting some silver things in my vagina and swabbing me with a Q-Tip. My clothes were taken for evidence. The only DNA from the man that was on me was one of his pubic sting of hair. They asked me if he had sex with me and I told them no. But by him not having sex with me, they said there was nothing that could be done.

I felt like the system had failed me again. I also felt like he should have been locked up for what he was doing to me. People knew he was having sex with a child. Nothing was ever said or done. After I had been swabbed at the hospital, I was taken to the police station. The police had him in one room. I was in another room. They asked me if he had sex with me and I told them no. I was so scared. The man had already told me not to tell anyone, so I didn't.

He had instilled so much fear in me, like the other two men had done. So, by the man not having had sex with me that day, the police said they had to let him go. That didn't keep the man from having sex with me; he continued to have sex with me even more and had sex with me in my anus so hard that I was bleeding from my anus and he had ruptured it. I went home crying that day and sat on the toilet. It looked like I had hemorrhoids, but it was part of my meat that came out of my anus. To this day, my anus is ruptured. He would have sex with me on my cycle.

Lord knows I didn't want any of those things to happen to me. I remember his aunt saying something about somebody had sex on her patio set and left blood there. I wanted to say something, but I didn't know how to. Some of his family members and friends knew that he was having sex with a child and no one ever said anything about it. Two of his friends used to let him bring me over to their house and have sex with me, and they never said anything. I thought it was normal and okay, because why would a knowing grown person just allow a grown man to have sex with a child and not say anything or protect that child?

He kept taking me to different motels and to people's houses to have sex with me. When he ended up getting a girlfriend, I thought that would stop him from having sex with me, but it didn't. His girlfriend found out that her boyfriend was having sex with me and she wanted to fight me over a grown man. She said that I had been sleeping with her man. I ended up catching trichomonas from the man having sex with me.

I was just an 11-year-old child. This grown man who was in his 30s knew better, but instead he was taking advantage of me, abusing my body, rupturing me, and raping me. I felt lost, hopeless, and helpless. Why was all of this happening to me? I was just a child who never said anything to those grown men. All I wanted to do was play outside with my cousins and friends, but I couldn't do that because of grown men raping and taking advantage of me and my mind.

My aunt didn't know about the first two men who had sex with me, but she knew about this man because she found my diary and she would find letters from him to mc, and from me writing him back. I felt like she should have had him locked up because it was proof that he had been having sex with me. My aunt said that she told me to leave him alone, and that was it. She had never done anything to protect me or have the man locked up.

The man kept having sex with me for years. He used to come and hang out at my aunt's house and act like nothing was going on or he wasn't in the wrong. He used to buy my aunt beer. I would look out of my window and he would wink his eye at me. He was also close to my mom and her husband, just like he was close to my family members.

He had started taking me to my mom and her husband's house to have sex with me. I was like, *why is my mom letting this grown man have sex with her child.* My mom had been scared and raped herself. You would have thought by her being my mom, she would have protected me and not allowed this man to be touching and having sex with her child. She told me that her mom didn't protect her and raise her. He would have sex with me while I was on my cycle at my mom's house. I was lost, hurt, confused, manipulated, raped, and taken advantage of by grown men who knew better. I was just a child.

I became pregnant at the tender age of 13 by my cousin's husband. One day, my cousin's husband had taken me over to their house. My little cousins were looking at me as I went into the room and their dad had closed the door. He had porn turned on and told me to sit on the bed and watch tv. I did. He got his Vaseline grease out and started stroking his penis, and he told me to take off my clothes. We laid on the bed and he got on top of me and slowly put his penis in my vagina.

It hurt so badly; he said it was going to be ok. He ended up cumming inside of me. I didn't know that I would become pregnant by him cumming in me. He told me to go to the bathroom and take a bath. I must have not gotten all the soap out of my vagina because when I left walking back to my aunt's house and I got by Spain's, my vagina started burning. It felt like splinters were poking my vagina; the pain was that bad.

I never told my aunt or anyone else what my cousin's husband had been doing to me. Like I said earlier, I wasn't believed the first time when the first man had sex with me and lied like he didn't, so who would believe me this time if I said my cousin's husband was having sex with me?

Sometimes, I would be so glad when it was time for me to go stay my two weeks at my dad's house, because I knew nothing bad would happen to me there. I just didn't like one of my stepsisters and her mom because one of the stepsisters and I used to fight sometime, and their mom was just firm. I wasn't used to that, so I would say she was mean.

I would have been better off living at my dad's house. One day, my dad, his wife, her two children, and I had gone on a church convention trip to Jolliet, Illinois. I was so hungry. I was too shy to go in the cooler to get me something to eat or drink, even though that was what it was there for. My stomach started hurting so badly. I still didn't get anything to eat or drink. We had made it to Jolliet. I finally had eaten something and started getting sleepy and tired, and just fell asleep.

I met a girl on the bus and her name was Iyonia. I told her that was a pretty name and I had never heard of that name before. We went to our hotel and checked in, and then went to church later that night. I remember sitting there on the bench falling asleep and my dad then kept waking me up. We stayed in Jolliet for a few days and then came back home. I would sleep most of the time because I was too shy to talk to anyone.

When we made it back to Grenada, MS, my dad and stepmom came into the room I had been sleeping in and asked me if I was pregnant and I didn't know I was pregnant, so I said, "No." My dad and his wife took me to the Health

Department the next day to have a pregnancy test done. The pregnancy test came back positive; I was pregnant. My dad, wife, the nurse, and I walked outside. The nurse talked to me about an abortion. I asked her what an abortion was because I didn't know.

I was 13 years old. I felt like I shouldn't have to have known about a baby or an abortion. The nurse told me that I would be killing my baby and if I wanted to have kids when I got older, my body could be messed up from having an abortion. When we got home from the Health Department, my dad came in the room and asked me who the baby's daddy was. I was scared to say something and plus I didn't know who the baby's daddy was because both men had been having sex with me.

After choosing not to abort my baby girl, I never lived at my dad's house again. I didn't know by him being into church if he was ashamed of his daughter being pregnant at 13. I felt like my dad gave up on me. I needed him the most then.

No abuse ever happened to me at my dad's house. All the abuse happened to me while in my aunt's care. Men had access to me. I didn't know who the baby daddy was because the neighborhood grandson and my cousin's husband had both been having sex with me. I wanted to tell my aunt and my cousin what was happening to me, but I didn't know how. Those grown men had instilled fear in me.

One day my cousin's husband told me to walk to Spain's and he would pick me up. My aunt told me that a lady of the family had said that she used to see me meeting my cousin's husband. I said *if she saw that, why didn't she say something or stop it?* I was a child, and he was a grown man who knew better than to be taking advantage of a 13-year-old child. He would take me to his house on Pine Hill. He would turn on porn and have me watch it. He would put Vaseline grease on his penis and then put some around my vagina. He then would start having sex with me. He would rub his penis up against me. He would tell me that it's okay and that he wasn't going to hurt me. He would see the expression on my face and tell me that everything would be okay.

Most of the time, he would pick me up at night. I guess so people wouldn't see him picking me up. One of my uncle's baby mamas said that she saw me in the car with him and she said she asked me what I was doing in the car with him and said I said nothing, and that he was just giving me a ride. I don't remember saying that. I do remember him taking me to Walmart one night to buy me things.

I never told any of my family member about what he had been doing to me. The secret could only stay a secret for so long. I was in the 7th grade when I became pregnant. I started showing. I would fall asleep in most of my classes because I would be so sleepy and tired. I still had classwork and homework to do. I really didn't talk much in school because I was shy. I had one best friend and a few friends in school. I would wear jackets and big T-shirts to hide my pregnancy. I was embarrassed. I had my daughter when I was in the 8th grade.

My cousin's husband was 33, and I was 13. One morning, he had sex with me in my aunt's living room while my aunt and her boyfriend were asleep. After having sex with me, he left. My aunt and boyfriend never knew about it.

I didn't feel loved by my family. I used to go with my cousin, her children, and husband shopping from time to time. My cousin never knew what her husband was doing to me. The three children of my cousin knew I was going in their mom and dad's room, but they never said a word to their mom or anyone else. I was hoping they would tell somebody, and I would be saved from the sexual abuse.

One Sunday, my dad had taken me to church with him, his wife, and my two stepsisters. I was in the Sunday school class. I was pregnant and showing a little, and I heard some girls say something about me being pregnant and laughing. I got up and ran out of the church. I was running and crying all the way to my aunt's house. To this day, my dad never knew why I got up from church and left. I was ashamed and embarrassed about being pregnant. I never wanted to be pregnant at a young age, but I was, and I wasn't going to kill my baby.

I wasn't being protected or safe at my aunt's house due to grown men taking advantage of me and having sex with me. I was safe at my dad's house. I was able to be a kid and have fun with my two stepsisters, when we weren't arguing or getting into it. One of my stepsisters and I would get into it from time to time, but I was still happy to be staying at my dad's house because there wasn't any abuse or anything going on over there.

I was too shy to talk. I had low self-esteem because of my smile. I hated my gap teeth. I stayed with my dad up until I became pregnant at the age of 13. I felt like my dad didn't love me either, because if he did, why would he send me to live with my aunt just because I got pregnant? I felt like he gave up on me. He still gave my aunt money for me, but that wasn't the same as being in my life and being there for me, especially when I needed him the most.

My cousin had been taking me back and forth to the doctor, and so did her husband. I was the only person in Middle School pregnant. As I started getting bigger and showing in my pregnancy at school, the coat that I would wear wasn't hiding the pregnancy anymore. The teachers never asked why this child was pregnant. I never talked to a school counselor, nor were social workers involved. I felt like the school system failed me as well as my family.

One day, mom and her husband had rushed me to the hospital because my water had broken. When I got to the hospital, I was vomiting a lot and was very sick from the pregnancy. The doctor had come into my room and started an IV on me. They gave me something for pain and vomit. They put this thing on my belly. It was to keep track of my contractions. I kept having sharp contractions. I didn't know what the hell was going on. I just knew I had pain that wouldn't stop. The doctor would come in every so often to stick his hand in my vagina to see how many centimeters I had dilated, and when I had finally gotten to nine centimeters, the doctor came in the room to deliver my baby.

My aunt and cousin were in the room when I got ready to deliver my baby. I was a child delivering a child. The doctor was telling me to push, but I didn't know how to push. The doctor said I almost died from having my baby because my body wasn't ready to be having a baby. I was a baby myself. I had pushed a few more times and there she came.

I named my daughter Iyonia Simoine Bankston. She weighed 6 lbs. and 7 oz. My friends came to the hospital to see me and my baby. They brought me gifts. One of my friend girls had brought me some ice cream from Wendy's. I couldn't take care of my baby because I was only

14 years old. I was still in the middle school. So, my cousin and aunt had to help take care of my baby and buy things like diapers, wipes, clothes, shoes, etc.

My baby started walking and was bowlegged. My cousin was joking, and she asked was my baby her husband's baby. I instantly started crying.

As my baby girl got older, she had started looking like my cousin's husband. One day, my cousin dropped me off at Wendy's where I worked, and she asked me if her husband and I had sex. I started crying and so did she. I told her, "Yes."

My aunt and her daughter suggested that a DNA test be done. I remember going to the courthouse with my cousin, her husband, my aunt, and my baby girl. The people had swabbed our mouth and sent the DNA swabs off.

The DNA test came back in the mail to my aunt's

address. I didn't know how to read the DNA test. My cousin read the DNA test, and it came back to be my cousin's husband's baby.

I lost my childhood again when I became pregnant at the tender age of 13 by my cousin's husband. I thought it was ok and normal to have sex with grown men, because that was all I knew. I didn't have anyone to talk to me about what was right and what was wrong, or to tell it if a man had tried to touch me down there to tell it.

I didn't know anything about raising a baby. I was never raised by my mom or my aunt. I just lived with my aunt. My dad didn't raise me. I basically raised myself. I was only 14 and wasn't able to get a job until I turned 16. As soon as I turned 16, I started working at Wendy's.

Wendy's was my first job. I was still in school. I had a lot of sleepless nights from being up with a baby. I don't know why my cousin's husband wasn't locked up after the DNA confirmed he was my baby's daddy. Those were *family secrets* that never came out.

As we went to the courthouse to take the DNA test, the judge never said anything like why is this child in here with this grown man having a DNA test done, nor did the people who swabbed our mouth. So, I feel like the system failed me. DHS wasn't involved, nor was social services. I feel like they looked at me like I was just a black girl having sex and out there in the streets getting pregnant. But that was not my case; I was being raped, manipulated, sexually assaulted, and being taken advantage of by grown men.

I felt very uncomfortable being around my cousin's husband. He would come to my aunt's house and act like nothing had ever happened. He never did for my baby girl. Even when the DNA test came back proving him to be my baby's daddy. My cousin didn't divorce him. He didn't acknowledge my baby. He would do for his kids that he had with my cousin, and that was it. My aunt and her daughter did everything for my baby. One of my cousins had given me a pair of shoes and some baby clothes.

Entering Domestic Violence 6

Still at age 14, another neighborhood guy started having sex with me. He was 23, and I was 14. One night I was walking down the street with my friend girl and the guy called me over. I went over and he had a bag of hot chips and a pickle. He called me in the house. I went in and he talked to me and manipulated me into having sex with him. So, for him to know that I liked hot chips and pickles, he had to have been watching me.

After having sex with him, he told me how beautiful I was and asked me if I wanted to be his girlfriend, just like the third man had asked me. I didn't know how to say no, and he instantly said I was his girlfriend. I was scared to tell anyone. The guy had started getting me to leave my aunt's house and to sneak out of the window to go stay with him. Two of my cousins used to ask me if they could go with me, and I would tell them no. I didn't want what was being done to me to be done to my cousins.

The man who had started having sex with me would tell me that everything was okay. He took me and my baby in. I was lost. I didn't know right from wrong because wrong and negativity were all that had been done to me and all I knew. He was living with his aunt at the time on Church Street which was around the corner from my aunt's house. He would get me to come over there to have sex with him.

One morning, I was laying on his aunt's couch and he had just got done having sex with me. He would connect the couches together so there would be room for the both of us to lie down. One of his friends came over and I was looking at his friend, wanting to say, *Help me!* I was scared and didn't know if his friend would tell him what I had just asked him to help me do, so I didn't say anything.

The guy was very verbally, physically, mentally, and emotionally abusive towards me. Some of his family members knew that he was having sex with me, but they didn't say anything. I was just being tossed around by all of those grown men. The guy had started jumping on me. He started calling me out of my name. He belittled me, cursed me, spit in my face, and told me I would never be anything in life. He told me that no one wanted me. I was so afraid of him. He would walk outside and shout and say, "Tanisha has AIDS." I felt so bad because he was lying on me and I knew I didn't have AIDS. At least I didn't think I did. I didn't know what I had because of grown men had been having sex with me.

As the years went by, I moved out of my aunt's house at the age of 17. I had gotten my first house, and it was right down the streets from my aunt. I was excited. I had not only gotten my first house, but I had gotten my first car at the age of 17. I was working part time at Wendy's. I had a car note, rent, bills, and two babies at the time.

My son's dad had gotten me pregnant when I was 17 years old. I was stressed out. He would take my car keys and my phone from me. When I would cook food, he would knock it out of my hand onto the floor and just curse me out and jump on me, even when I was pregnant with my son. He would get so drunk and not show up in my car to pick me up from work. I would have to ride with other people, and they would have to drop me off at my aunt's house or my house.

I worked a lot of late nights, getting off at 2 AM. After getting pregnant with my daughter and having her, my dad said he would take me to get on some birth control. I remember him paying for me some patches. As I would go to my son's aunt's house, he had convinced me to take off my birth control patch because he said that he wanted a baby by me. I ended up getting pregnant by him. After getting pregnant, he started saying my baby wasn't his baby. I knew that I hadn't slept with anybody else.

I was so afraid to talk to other guys. I was in a

domestic violence, abusive relationship with my son's dad. He threw my, and my kids', clothes in a sewage and in the garbage can all because he said he felt like doing it.

He was a bad alcoholic. Later, he started driving trucks for swift trucking company. He told me I better not hang up the phone because if I did, he would jump on me when he got home. He was so jealous. I would be very tired and sleepy trying to not hang up the phone because I knew he was serious about jumping on me. He had done it so many times. He didn't have to worry about me talking to other guys because he had so much fear, control, and power over me from all that he had done to me.

Everything in my house was mine because it was my house. He was just living with me. He had given one of his sisters my big screen tv, my kids' bedroom set, and my kids' Wii system. I went to her to ask for my things back and she said she didn't have them. I knew she did because I had seen them in her house. I used to go over to his sister's house. I was hurt from seeing my furniture in his sister's house. I was later garnished for my furniture that his sister had of mine. I felt so stupid. I was paying for furniture that I didn't even have and that his sister had of mine. She still has my kid's bedroom set to this day.

From time to time, I wouldn't stay at my house and would stay at my aunt's house because I was tired of my son's dad jumping on me. He would come and try to get me out of her house to curse at me and talk crazy to me through the window. Some of my family members knew what was going on. I guess they were scared of him, too. So, nothing was ever said or done to him. I remember calling the police. He ended up with two domestic violence charges against me.

I used to cry when he would come to my aunt's house and yell at me through the window and call me all kinds of bad names. Guys at school would try to talk to me, but I was scared to talk to them, and they would say, "Tanisha don't like younger guys, she likes older guys." I was in fear from the grown men having sex with me and being beaten by my son's dad and didn't know how to get out of it or tell anyone.

He was jealous. He didn't want to work. He had stopped driving trucks for Swift Trucking company. I was having to pay all the bills by myself and take care of two small children, plus pay a car note. I ended up studying for my driver's licenses and got them. I graduated from high school when I was 18 years old. I started going to Holmes Community College in fall of August 2007 after I graduated high school. I was so proud of myself because I was the first out of my immediate family to go to college.

I majored in nursing. I didn't get into the nursing program. I took the ACT and scored a sixteen, and that was all you needed to get into the LPN program. I had taken all of my basic courses, so when I did get into the nursing program, I would already have them out the way.

One day, my eldest brother had found out about my son's dad jumping on me and beating me. My brother was at my house and my son's dad had started walking through the house and knocking things over. My high school diploma was sitting on the shelf and he knocked it down and it got wet. My son's dad had started cursing and talking crazy to me. My brother had gotten a rusty gun that he had found under the chair on the porch and went in my house and asked my son's dad did he hit me. He didn't. My brother had hit my son's dad in the head with the rusty gun and started beating him with it.

I was crying and screaming because they both were fighting. My brother was going to kill him. My brother ended up slipping on the blood that was on the floor from my son's dad's head. My son's dad had gotten on top of my brother and started choking him. I tried to pull him off of my brother. I had blood all over my white t-shirt. They both were tired from fighting. *I called the police.*

A police officer came and took me and my brother to jail. My son's dad was taken to the hospital where he had to get staples in his head. I told the police that I didn't do anything and that I was just trying to break my brother and my son's dad up, but he didn't believe me because I had so much blood on me like I too had been fighting.

I was handcuffed and taken to the police station. I was taken to jail for nothing. My picture and fingerprints had been taken. I was crying. I was taken to the back, where I had to take off my clothes and take a shower. The water was so hard. I had to put on an orange jail house shirt, orange pants, a sports bra, and some orange shoes. I was taken to the back with other inmates. I was brought a tray. The food looked nasty. The mashed potatoes were hard. The Kool-Aid was too sweet. I didn't eat or drink anything. I gave my tray to a lady. I was praying that I didn't have to be in jail much longer. I had always heard the stories about jail and seen them on tv.

I was 18 years old when I got locked up. The doors slimmed, and I jumped. I was crying so badly. The inmates were telling me that I was going to be okay and that they knew my mother. My mother had been in and out of jail and prison most of my life. When I was able to get a phone call, I called my dad and asked him if he would come and get me out of jail. He said he would come and get me from jail, but he would never come and get me if I ever were to get locked up again. I sat in jail for eight hours until my dad finally came and got me.

I was in so much shock from seeing all that blood on the floor at my house. I had gone to my house and started mopping up the blood with some bleach and hot water. The smell of the blood was so horrible. After my brother got released from jail, he had nowhere to live. He had moved out of his grandparent's house when he turned 18 years old. My son's dad didn't want my brother living with us, so I told my brother he couldn't live there. My son's dad had so much power and control over me.

Later, my lights and gas had gotten turned off. My brother and I slept in my cold house in the bed together. I was so hurt on the inside telling my brother he couldn't live with us. My brother ended up getting his own place on Levee St. I started staying down at my brother's house, especially when my son's dad would jump on me and put me and my kids out of my own house. My brother ended up meeting some so-called friends who stayed down to his house all the time. His so-called friends had turned him against his family, they told him that his family was no good to him. We stopped talking behind them turning him against his family. They had power over my brother like my son's dad had over me. They told him that they were his family.

MY PAIN IS MY POWER

Losing My Eldest Brother 7

My mom had moved in with my eldest brother. He didn't know how to cook. All he knew how to cook were Tyson Chicken Strips out of the bag. I would go down to my brother's house from time to time. We didn't really talk much. One day, my sister and I were walking up the street together and our brother was in front of us, and we had started picking with him. My brother too was shy. Another day, my brother was walking up the street and I passed by him and didn't stop or blow the horn. I was mad at him for allowing his so-called friends to turn him against his family.

My brother had dropped out of school in the 11th grade. He went and took the GED test and he passed on his first try with high scores. He enrolled at Holmes Community College for a few semesters. He would walk to school. My brother was determined, but had started hanging with the wrong crowd. He had a job and was working at Bains Manufacturer. He was doing so good for himself until it came to his friends. He changed, and they changed him.

One day, I was driving my car, and I saw my brother walking. I never thought that would be my last time seeing my brother alive. We were on bad terms; so, I didn't get a chance to apologize to my brother for picking with him or to tell him that I love him. My brother was born on July 13, 1989. He died on September 13, 2008. He died when he was 19 years old. He never got a chance to enjoy his life. Just when he started to enjoy his life, he lost his life.

I remember being at Walmart and hearing the ambulance, and I had a gut feeling that something wasn't right. I then got a phone call saying that my brother had been in a wreck and that I should get to the hospital. I did. I saw my brother laying on a stretcher. He was looking at me like *Sis, please don't let me die*. I asked what had happened, and I was told that he had been in a wreck. I was told he was pulled over by a police officer for swerving in the road.

My brother didn't know how to drive. I don't understand why the man who was having sex with me let him drive his car. The hospital never knew that my brother had chewed an 8 ball of cocaine. I was also told that the guy in the car with my brother, which was one of my aunt's boyfriend, had given him an orange soda which had a lot of acid in it, which only made the acid in his stomach worse. My brother had started having a seizure from the cocaine that he chewed.

The doctors never knew that my brother had cocaine in his system. About 30 mins later, we were sitting in the waiting room and the doctor came and told us to go to the Chaplain Hall. We knew then that my brother had passed away. My mom came into the hospital and they told her what had happened and that her son had just died.

She fell to the floor crying, and they had to pick her up and put her in a wheelchair. The doctor let us go in the back to see my brother by pairs of two. I was looking at my brother's dead body lying on the table. He was skinny, but his body has swollen. He didn't even get to live his life.

I felt so bad because I didn't get to say goodbye to my brother, and we were on bad terms. I was told by one of the friends of the family he called the ambulance because his so-called friends left him outside to die. I was told that my brother had told his so-called friends what he had done and they said they didn't call the ambulance because they were scared they would go to jail. I felt like they all should have gone to jail for letting my brother lay outside on the ground to die. He ended up dying.

My brother's so-called friends came to the hospital, and then they left. They went back to his house to get their things out. They took a lot of my brother's stuff like his clothes, shoes, gun, and money. I blamed myself for my brother's death for years. I felt like if I had stopped my car and had given him a ride, he would still be alive.

Some of my co-workers from Wendy's would come to my house to try to take me out to eat, but I wouldn't leave the house because I was so sad and depressed about losing my brother. It took a toll on me; I didn't know what to do. We already didn't grow up together or have a bond. It was like we were just starting to get to know each other and losing him without knowing him. I really went into a depression mode and didn't come out. I let my brother's so-called friends, who turned him against his family, keep us from talking.

MY PAIN IS MY POWER

Ending Domestic Violence 8

I moved out of my house on Pearl St. to a different house. I moved to an apartment on Main Street. I stayed there for a few years until I was evicted because of my son's dad showing out in the apartment. He would always get drunk and jump on me and break my furniture. He would jump on me in front of my kids. He was always worried about me cheating on him and talking to somebody else. I was scared to even blink at another guy. I would call the police and the landlord had gotten tired of it.

One night, the landlord came over and told me that he could not keep having the police come to his apartments. He told me that I had to move out of his apartment. I was so heartbroken and hurt behind it. I was still working at Wendy's part time, making $5.35 an hour, and going to

Holmes Community College. My son's dad wasn't working. I was the only one working and in debt. I was taking out student loans to help pay up my rent and bills. There was no way I could have paid all of those bills by myself with two small kids, bills, and a car note.

After being evicted, I moved on to Thomas St. I met an older man who was nice to me. I had never had a man be nice to me and not try to use me, take advantage of me, or manipulate me into having sex with him. One day he came to the car wash where I was washing my car. He said to me that he detailed cars and that he would wash my car for me. We had exchanged numbers and became friends.

One night, he called me and we met up. I left walking from Holmes Community College and he picked me up. We went and got a hotel. We had sex that night. He was in his 30s and I was 19 years old. That was the first time I had ever cheated on or messed around on my son's dad.

I wouldn't call my son's dad and I being in a relationship. I say it was trafficking. I couldn't leave him, no matter how I tried to. He would always show up when I tried leaving him. I would call the police and he would end up with domestic violence charges against me for jumping on me.

One night, my son's dad was in my house waiting for me to come in. He had turned all the lights off in my house and was hiding. I don't know if he was going to kill me or not. I had the police sitting outside waiting for me to go into my house to get some clothes. As I went in the house, my son's dad came out of my room. I guess he saw the police lights, so he ran out of the back door.

I really had no one to talk to, so I ended up getting close to the older guy who stayed two doors down from me. He listened my problems when I needed someone to talk to. I wanted out of the domestic violence, abusive relationship. I asked the man, whom I had become friends with, what should I do. He said to leave and call the police, but it was easier said than done, because I had done all of that. I was scared of him.

I knew I had to leave my son's dad when one morning I was getting ready for work and he hit me on my leg with an iron baseball bat for nothing. I went to work that morning. I was working at the hospital and I cried. The crazy thing was my son's dad also worked at the hospital. I hated seeing him. I told my coworkers what was going on and they told me to leave him. Once again, it wasn't that easy. I started trying to find a way out of that relationship. He would always jump on me in front of my two kids. They would be grabbing me like I grabbed my mom, when she would get jumped on by men.

One day, he came home. He was mad. My kids and I went into my bedroom and I locked the door. He was saying to unlock the door, and we were screaming and crying. He picked up my son's bike and threw it at the door, trying to break in. He left a hole in the landlord's door of my bedroom. I said to myself; *I have to get out of this domestic violence relationship, because if I don't, he is going to kill me and my kids won't have a mom.* So, I met a guy through Facebook. We became friends and started talking. The guy was stocky, strong, and a bodyguard. I felt safe and protected by him being around. He protected me and my kids. I asked him if he wanted me to tell my son's dad that we were talking, and he said he didn't care.

So, I went home one morning and told my son's dad that I was seeing someone else. He didn't take it well and started throwing and breaking things in my house. He took my furniture and left my doors opened. He bust my TVs and a lot of my other stuff. He poured beer in my bed and on the floor.

The guy who I had met through Facebook, and I started dating. He stayed some nights with me. I knew he would and could protect me. I felt safe with him being around. My kids liked him a lot. He interacted with them and showed them love.

I was still friends with my neighbor, and he started brain washing me and manipulating me. He had me believing that the guy was out cheating on me. After work, the guy would go workout at the gym at night. For Valentine's Day, the guy bought me a rose and a teddy bear. I was so happy with the gifts, because I have never had anyone give me anything or be nice to me.

Things didn't work out with me and the new guy that I had been dating. I had been so traumatized from my past and being manipulated and taken advantage by grown men. I didn't know a good man when I had one. He stopped coming over my house. I really liked him a lot. He said I was jealous and insecure. I felt like my neighbor liked the fact that we weren't together anymore because it was his way of coming to my house whenever he wanted to.

The guy that I had met on Facebook was my way out of the domestic violence relationship. I left my son's dad when I was 23 years old. That was a long time to be locked up in prison, because that is exactly where I felt. My mind was in prison. I dealt with my son's dad for nine years. From the age of 14 to the age of 23, until I found a way to escape that toxic abusive domestic relationship through meeting the guy on Facebook.

MY PAIN IS MY POWER

My First Love

I never gave myself time to heal after leaving my son's dad and when I stopped talking to the bodyguard. One day, I was at Tally's and this guy had asked me for my phone number and I said, "No." Then, the next night, I had seen him at a gas station. He asked me for my number again, so I gave it to him. I was shocked that this handsome guy was asking this torn, scared girl for her phone number.

I had low self-esteem from all the trauma I had endured as a child. My smile was ugly and the things that I went through, especially being beaten up by my son's dad. The guy came over to my house the next day during his lunch break. I used to tell my neighbor everything. I told him that my new guy friend was coming over. He didn't like that, and he was in my house trying to have sex with me. I told him to leave, and he didn't want to leave. He left right when my new guy friend got there.

My new friend and I were talking. I was so happy to finally meet somebody who I could have a real relationship with, to fall in love with, and live happily ever after. At least that was what I thought. I fell in love with this new guy when we met at his cousin's house. Yes! I believe in love at first sight because I fell in love with him when I first met him. We had started spending time together.

One night, I went to his cousin's house. We stood outside, hugging and kissing. I can say that was my first real kiss. The guy smelled good, looked good, and dressed nicely. It almost felt like a dream. We laughed and talked for a while until I went home. He was living with his parents. We would stay up texting and talking on the phone. On our first date, we went to Captain D's in Greenwood, MS. I was so quiet and nervous. I didn't know what to say or what to talk about. I couldn't believe I was on my first real date. I liked him so much.

After going out to eat, we came back to my house, and he stayed the night. We laid in my bed and I asked him if he wanted to move in with me and be my boyfriend, not even really knowing him. I was already in love with him, but he wasn't in love with me, and he told me he wasn't ready for a relationship, and I should have listened.

I was told he had been messing with a lady. I went and talked to the lady. She told me to leave him alone, and that I was too sweet for him and that he will break my heart. Damn! She was right when I thought she was wrong. I thought she was jealous, but the whole time she was trying to help save me from a heartbreak.

I moved him in with me. He broke my heart. He cheated on me. He had never stopped talking to other women. After going through his phone seeing him text and talk to other women, I confronted him and put him out several times, but he begged me to let him come back. I was weak for him. I was lonely. One night, I had asked him if he had ever been locked up and he said yes. I asked what for and he said that he didn't want to talk about it, so I left it alone. Come to find out, he was a registered sex offender. He said that he was set up, and some stuff happened.

I neglected my kids for him, just as my mom did me for men. I would drop my kids off at my aunt's house just to be with that man and allow him to lay up in my house to smoke cigarettes and play his video games. My relationship with my kids changed when I met him. I stopped paying attention to my kids and put all of my attention on my first real boyfriend. My oldest daughter was 9 years old, and my son was 6 years old. I was 24 years old when I started talking to the new guy. I had changed. My children noticed the change in me. My behavior and attitude changed my children's and my relationship.

I was so blinded by love. My boyfriend never loved me like I loved him. All I wanted was to be loved and cared about by a man. I loved my children, but I neglected them, and I stopped paying attention to them. My boyfriend and I never really spent much time together or take my kids places. He would always want to go to his cousin or friend's house to play his video game when he got off work, but he was really texting and talking to other women.

One day, he told me he was going out of town with some of his guy friends and I said okay. So, he went to Memphis. A girl called my phone that night and told me that he was at her house and she told me all the things that he had done to her. I cried. I heard him lying in her bed, snoring. The girl woke him up that night and made him leave. He made it to my house the next morning. I told him that he had to leave. I had told him all the things that happened to me, and he didn't care. He just wanted a place to lay his head and to be closer to his job in Grenada, MS. He kept convincing me to let him stay with me by telling me he was sorry and that he would never cheat on me again, but he lied, and he kept cheating on me and talking to other women. It was like he had a habit of talking to women and couldn't stop.

I cried night and day over this man who cared nothing for me; he only used me. He didn't love me like I loved him. I neglected my two children to be with a man who cared nothing for me and clearly nothing for my children. We dated for two years.

I called my neighbor and told him what was going on. The neighbor and I were still friends, my neighbor watched my house while I went to work. I was still working at the hospital. I worked 12-hour shifts from 7 a.m. to 7 p.m. My neighbor would tell me that my boyfriend would come home right before it was time for me to get off work. One night, somebody broke into my house. I blamed my boyfriend because I told him if he would have been home more, instead of being gone all the time, nobody would have been able to break into my house. They stole our pit bull puppy, my flat screen tv, my son's Play Station game system, the top comfort sheet off my bed, and more stuff.

I was heartbroken. That wasn't the first time somebody had broken into my house, this was the second time; my kids and I were scared to live in our house, because I knew somebody had been watching my house and I didn't know who was doing it. I wanted to get revenge for him cheating on me, to get him to stop and just to love me and only me. So, my neighbor told me to create a Facebook page about him being a registered sex offender and I did it. I was so hurt. I felt so bad, but I didn't think about it hurting my boyfriend, because I was the one hurting from being cheated on.

He had called me and told me to take off of Facebook. He said he knew I had created that page. I denied it. He told a police officer. The police officer called me and told me to take the post down and if I didn't, my ex-boyfriend said that he was going to press charges against me for creating a fake page.

I told my neighbor what was being said, he said he deserved it. No matter what, I felt like he didn't deserve that. I was just trying to get his attention. I told him that my neighbor had told me to create that page and do that to him and he said, "Tanisha, I still can't believe you would do something like that."

I told him, "I only wanted him to stop cheating on me and to love me for me." All I wanted was for someone to love me. All my life, I had been mistreated and abused. He said, "Well you never have to worry about me again."

I got my first job when I was 16 years old. I worked at Wendy's for 7 years. I left Wendy's and went to the Hospital called UMMC of Grenada, MS. While working at the hospital, I researched and looked up what do you have to do to become a Certified Pharmacy Technician. I ended up paying to get my temporary license to work in a pharmacy for 1 year until I became fully certified. I worked at UMMC for 3 years and 7 months. I left there because my kids were small, and I was working 12-hour shifts from 7 a.m. to 7 p.m.

I left the hospital to go to work at Walgreens. When I applied to work for Walgreens, I applied to work in the pharmacy. I had to take a test before I could get hired in the pharmacy. I had taken the test. The store manager told me that I barely passed the test. I didn't care if I barely passed the test. I passed, so that's all that should have mattered. But by me being a black girl, I felt like he didn't think I should have scored high enough to pass the test. He told me that he didn't have any openings in the pharmacy, but I could apply for the front store as a cashier. So I did. I needed a job, and I had bills and small children who I had to take care of.

A Caucasian girl came into Walgreens and asked if they were hiring. The manager told the girl that he had an opening in the pharmacy. She applied for it and he hired her in the pharmacy. Remember, I just said that I had applied for the pharmacy, and he told me that he didn't have any openings. I had my associate's degree in Pre-Nursing. I had medical background experience from working at the hospital, taking medical classes through Holmes Community College, and being in the EMT program. I had my temporary licenses to work in a pharmacy for up to a year before I had to be licensed. I felt discriminated against because she got hired in the pharmacy and I didn't.

One day, a Caucasian lady had to have surgery and was going to be out. The store manager and a shift lead had called me in the office to tell me that I would be working in the pharmacy only to the lady came back to work. I said ok. Deep down I was saying to myself that I am only being used. I was the only African American person working in the pharmacy. I went through a lot working in the pharmacy. A lot of racial stuff was said. I just ignored it and kept working.

Then, one day, the manager's wife came in while I was singing, "Do the Ratchet" by Lil' Boosie. She asked me if I had called her rachet and I told her no, because I didn't. The next day the manager called me in the office to ask me if I had called a customer ratchet and I told him no.

He said that rachet was a derogatory word, and that he was going to have to let me go. See, the customer was the manager's wife. They both felt some type of way. The manager never had a problem with me singing before, but that day he had a problem because it was his wife; so, I was escorted out of the store by the pharmacist like I was a criminal who had done something.

I tried to buy something before leaving and they would not let me buy anything. I felt some type of way because I had never been fired from a job or ever had a problem on a job. I have always been bullied on every job that I had.

After being fired from Walgreens, I googled and found information on how to become a certified pharmacy technician. I studied for the exam and found where you can take your exam and paid and registered to take my exam and went and took and passed my exam. I had previously failed my pharmacy exam three times while working at Walgreens. I guess that was God's way of saying your time and season are up from working here.

I applied to work for Walmart in the pharmacy. I never got hired. I would always see new faces there and people who weren't even certified who were working back in the pharmacy. I took my resume in. I graduated from high school when I was 18 years old in May 2007. I attended Holmes in August 2007. I majored in Nursing. I had started the EMT program in January 2010. I ended up withdrawing from the program. I had some things going on with my mom. I graduated from Holmes Community College in December 2010 with my Associate's Degree. I kept going to college. I ended up going to Mississippi Valley State for Social Work.

My kids were small at the time, so I wasn't able to attend some of the classes they required. So, I got all the basic classes that I could get online. I then went to Delta State University to get some more of the classes that I could get for Social Worker. I wanted to be a Social Worker to help kids like myself and not fail them like the system had failed me. I was told there was an opening in the electronics department. I was asked if I could come in the next day for orientation, and I said yes. There it was. I had gotten hired. Not for the department I was certified to work in, but I was in the door.

The department manager had started picking with me for nothing. I would go to the store manager and nothing would get done. So, I had started calling Corporate. They talked to the department manager, but that didn't stop her from picking with me and saying bad things to me. See, I am a fighter, not a quitter. I didn't get the jobs I had applied for, but I got a job.

I left Walmart in January 2020 to focus on my business. I am in Financial Services. I enjoy helping families set up a financial game plan, saving money, and getting out of debt. I want to help others like myself. I had a rough childhood. Not only had I been raped, sexually assaulted, and taken advantage of by grown men, but I lost my oldest brother in 2008 due to drug overdose. I should have taken a break from college after I lost my brother, but I kept going and started failing. I ended up with a lot of student loan debt due to having to pay all of my bills by myself because my son's dad didn't want to work and I was only working part time at Wendy's.

MY PAIN IS MY POWER

Don't Move Too Fast If You Aren't Ready

I went out one night to my cousin's club, and I saw a guy. He looked good. After the club, I went home. My ex was supposed to come and see me that night, and he didn't. The guy had started liking a lot of my pictures on Facebook. I in boxed him and said *I see your liking a lot of my pictures* and he said yes and wanted to know if he could get to know me. I said yes. I was lonely, hurt, and sad.

I started talking to the guy. He came to my house one day, and we talked, and he wanted to get to know me, but I was still hurt and in love with my ex. I told the guy I wasn't ready for a relationship. He said he could help me get over my ex, but I moved this guy in when I know I shouldn't have. I wasn't ready for a relationship, but I was lonely. I started cheating on him.

I dated this guy for 5 years and during that time I became pregnant. We have a 3-year-old baby girl together now named Khloe Grace. He proposed to me. He and I decided to have a baby since he didn't have any kids. I wanted to give him his first child, but he started seeing a girl at his job and she became pregnant with his first child. I was hurt to where I cried. I wanted to give him his first child, but another woman had already done that. Our relationship really was rocky. His dad had gotten sick. He went out there to help his mom with his dad. I got lonely and seeked out. I got on POF, a dating site.

My Second Love

I met a younger guy. We talked every night and day on the phone. I begged my ex-fiancé to come home because I was lonely. He didn't come home most of the time. He said that I could come to his mom's house, but I had my kids and my newborn baby.

One day, this new guy came to see me at Walmart with his mom and his three kids. I went to his house one night, supposedly taking him some detox tea that I had made for him since he was a truck driver. I was so ready to see him, and I forgot to grab the detox tea. We talked and laid on his air mattress. He had just moved into his trailer. We had sex that night. I fell for him, then came back home. After having sex with him, I feel in love with him. I think it was more LUST than LOVE. We continued to talk on the phone every day and night. We became very close.

My ex-fiancé called me one morning as I was on my way home from my new lover's house and told me that his dad had passed. I was hurt behind that. But I knew that would change things between me and my lover. I kept seeing this new guy. I went home one day and told my ex-fiancé I couldn't do this anymore. I told him that I was seeing a guy. I'm sure I hurt him like my ex hurt me.

My boyfriend and I have been dating now for three years. I look forward to what the future holds for us. We don't have any children of our own together. We have been talking about having a baby. He has three children of his own. I have three children of my own.

Feeling Like The Black Sheep of My Family   14

I feel like I am the black sheep of my family. My family and I are not close. I want a relationship with my family. I have a lot of incest in my family to where some of my cousins had been coming into my room late at night, when my aunt would go out to the clubs and play in my panties. I would move their hands and they would still keep coming back into my room.

Some of my cousins used to pick on me when I was young. I was teased and bullied growing up. I didn't know how to stand up for myself. I didn't smile a lot because of my gap teeth. My aunt, who raised me, had a son (who has now passed away) who used to come into my room and go into my pants and put my foot up against his penis to masturbate. He had done this for a long time. I never told anyone because I wasn't believed when I was raped at 5 or 6 years old, so why would someone believe me now.

The family secrets that are kept hidden do come up to surface. I wondered why me. Why were all of these things happening to me? Why was I the one getting touched and taken advantage of by grown men? Why did I get raped?

Since the year of 2000. I have lost so many family members. Mary Alice, Big mama, Mr. Melvin, Laquenda, Nay, Andrae, Pig, Desmond, Neka, Maine, Kela, and Lil Mike.

I want to break the generational curses off this family. I am different. Before my aunt Mary Alice passed away, she said that the world would change. She was a Jehovah's Witness. She would take my cousin and I to church with her all the time. I enjoyed going to church at a very young age.

I want to become a motivational speaker. I am a business owner. I want to travel the world and talk to people and tell my story. I want to tell my story about how I overcame all that happened to me and how I am still standing. I am a survivor.

I want to move away from Grenada, MS. I am coming out of my shell. I am getting closer to God. I want to understand Him and learn His Word. I am a Licensed Insurance Agent for Primerica. I am a certified pharmacy technician. I want to meet new people and grow and expand my business.

I want to just live and have a normal life. I just want to be happy. I am overcoming Fear and stepping out on Faith.

MY PAIN IS MY POWER

I have found my purpose in life and that is to help others. I ask myself, *Why am I chosen to still be here despite of all trauma and things that I have gone though in life?* God answered and said that I have a purpose to help others like myself.

Why did I have to go through all that I went through? I have always had low self-esteem as a child and growing up. I was bullied in school and even on jobs because of my last name. Kids would say that I liked grown men, and that I dated grown men, but they didn't know my story or know that I had been taken advantage of by those grown men.

I didn't talk to anyone in school because of my smile. My teeth were jacked up. I had a really big gap and spaced-out teeth. I had to wait until I got out of high school and pay for my braces. I remember writing my dad a letter saying, "All I want for Christmas was some braces." That never happened! I was shy and afraid to talk to my dad. My dad never knew any of the bad things that happened to me as a child. Once my gap closed, my teeth changed my appearance.

I have a hard time focusing, concentrating, and staying on task. I react without thinking. I have always helped my family, but I can't get anyone to help me. I feel like my dad gave up on me when I became pregnant, and that was when I needed him the most. I was safe at my dad's house. Nothing bad happened to me there, but at my aunt's, all the bad things happened to me.

I want to get surrounded by positive people because all my life I have been surrounded by negativity to where it had rubbed off on me. When somebody positive came into my life, I didn't know how to act or react because I saw life differently because of men abusing my body.

I never thought I would be taking care of my mom. My mom didn't take care of me or raise me. I don't know what it's like being a mother, really. I feel like I am doing my best at taking care of my children. Everything I know, I had to learn on my own.

I don't think I have a fair life. I pray for everyone and forgive everyone who has done something to me or harmed me in my life. I feel like I am too forgiving. I want to stop being so nice and just open and speak my mind.

I worry about myself sometimes. I don't want to turn to medication when there is a God. I don't want to get hooked on medication. I have tried different kinds of medicine and they do not help. Seems like with my nighttime medicine, I had more nightmares on it than off it. I'm just going to keep praying and talking to God. God, I need you and I love you.

Finding The Tanisha
I Was Born To Be

I have been introduced to supportive groups on Facebook. I started posting and sharing my life story. People started reaching out to me, asking me to speak on their podcast and radio stations. I was glad to do so, but was also nervous. I did my first speaking on July 3, 2020 on a radio talk show called NAASCA which stands for National Association Adult Survivors of Child Abuse. As I was speaking, it was a relief off of me. But let me tell you, it opened a can of worms with my family.

Some of my family members didn't like it when I first spoke about my childhood and my past. Nobody ever asked me if I was ok. I was ok when I started opening and speaking about my life. I shared my story on Facebook. I went live about how I felt and opened up more. A lady commented on my post and asked me if I would like to speak on her podcast, and I was glad to do so.

Remember earlier in my book I talked about wanting to overcome fear, be happy, become a speaker. I had the chance to do those things. I spoke again on July 13, 2020, on "Your Voices of Hope." The more I spoke, the more confident I became. I spoke again on October 28, 2020 at "Re-Discover Me" and on "Let's Talk About It." On December 11, 2020 I was a guest speaker on "Ask a Sex Abuse Survivor." I was later asked to become a domestic violence advocate. I was honored.

My life has been changing even more since I started working on getting closer to God. I have been fasting, praying, and seeking God. I have always had this pain in my heart and back from a broken heart and all the hurt that I have endured. One day, God came to me and said, "My child, get up in front of your boyfriend and praise me and I will remove all of your pain."

I was scared and afraid and I had told my boyfriend the message that God had said to me, and he told me that if God told me those things that I had to do them. And when I tell you that the next day I got up and started praising God, a sense of relief came upon me. I started speaking in tongues and shouting. The pain that I had in my heart and back for years was gone. All the heartaches were gone as well.

That was the very first moment I started realizing and seeing that God was real. All God wants us to do is have faith and believe. I put my faith and belief in God, but let me tell you something, when the devil sees you trying to do good and be on the right track; he will come after you and use every trick in the book to keep you from being who God says you are supposed to be and serving God.

I lost my inner voice when I was raped at the tender age of 5 or 6 years old. I found my inner voice at the age of 32. My inner voice was trapped for twenty-seven years. God came to me and told me that I will never forget my past, so stop trying to bury it and make it go away because this is my story, and I am alive to still stand and tell it.

I spoke again on March 22, 2021 on "So LUX Life Podcast." I got some backlash again from some of my family members saying if you're going to tell the whole story tell it right, saying my little stinky panties went to everybody, being called bitches, whores, sluts, saying I willingly gave my body up to men. I told the lady who was saying all of those things about me that her son was having sex with me and messing with me when I was younger, too. I asked her if she thought I was lying about that and she said if she didn't know me personally, she would believe me. I told her, "I was going to pray for her and her family."

She said, "Don't bother to pray for us, after all you and your children are not together, so save your fake ass prayers and use them bouncing off the ceiling prays for ya'll."

True, my teenagers and I aren't in the same household right now. My teenagers both fought me twice. My daughter fought me for trying to discipline her. She was being disrespectful to me as well. They are teenagers and they don't want to listen to me. I allowed my teenagers to instill fear in me. I ran from them and my house. My son is staying at his dad's house. My oldest daughter is staying at my house with my uncle. She will be graduating in May 2021 and going off to College.

I didn't know how to discipline my kids when I was younger, but now that I am grown and older, "I do." My boyfriend took my baby and me in. We came up here to live at his house. I had to find myself.

MY PAIN IS MY POWER

My Oldest Daughter, Iyonia 19

I became a teen mom at the tender age of 14. I didn't know how to be a mom. I was just a child myself. My daughter and I were like sisters. I didn't know how to change a diaper. I had to learn how to do that. I didn't know how to properly clean around my baby naval. A nurse had to come to the house after I was discharged from the hospital. She taught me how to clean around my baby naval. She told me to use a Q-Tip and put a little drop of alcohol on it and rub it around her naval to clean it. There were times when I had put a little too much on the Q-tip and it had gotten into my baby naval. She would scream and cry.

My aunt and her daughter had to help me take care of my baby because I was only 14 and didn't have any money. I couldn't work at the age of

14. I had to wait two more years before I could get a job. The school had sent work home with me before I got ready to leave. I had lots of homework to do that I had to get done and turned in. I had a newborn baby that had to be taken care of. I was so tired and sleepy from being up all night with my baby.

She would cry a lot and throughout the night when she was hungry. I would have to get up and go make her a bottle. I would have to boil the water so it could get warm and pour sterile water into her bottle and pour power into it and then shake it and put it back in a pot of water until it was warm. I would have to feed my baby and burp her and then put her back to sleep. My baby slept in the bed with me most nights. She had a baby crib right next to my bed, but I didn't trust putting her in the crib, letting her sleep throughout the night because I had heard of how babies die in a crib.

My baby was my everything. I love her so much. I remember for her first birthday; my cousin's girlfriend had made her a birthday cake. She had a big piece. I only have a few baby pictures of my baby. She started Head Start when she was 3 years old. I was 17 years old and still in school. I remember putting my baby girl on the Head Start bus and then getting on the bus myself. Wow! I remember having to go to meetings at the Head Start. I had to grow up fast. It wasn't that I wanted to grow up fast. My childhood was stolen from me.

My daughter was diagnosed with a disorder called Narcolepsy with Cataplexy when she was 9 years old. One-night, Iyonia was sitting on the couch eating a slice of pizza when she had suddenly fallen asleep with the slice of pizza in her mouth. I was like that isn't normal. I had to wake her up. The next day I called her pediatrician. I told them that I wanted to bring her in to get seen because she had fallen asleep with a slice of pizza. She was snoring. I took her to the doctor, and they referred her to Select Specialty Hospital in Jackson, MS.

The doctor there said he wanted to do a sleep study on my Iyonia. We went home and went back to Jackson the next week. The doctor told me to not to let her fall asleep and to try to keep her awake on the way there so her test results would be accurate. We lived 1 hour and 45 minutes away from Jackson, MS. It was very difficult and hard keeping her awake.

We finally made it to the hospital. The technicians came into the room and talked to me and my daughter. They explained to us what they would be doing, and they hooked all kinds of cords to her head, on her legs, and put oxygen in her nose. They told her to lie down around 8 PM. When she laid down, she instantly fell asleep like within 30 mins. The next morning, the sleep technicians came in and unhooked her from all the cords. She had sticky white paste in her head from the stuff they had put in her hair. She had to have the sleep study done for two days.

After the sleep study was done, we were discharged. The doctor called me when the test results came in. We drove back to Jackson. The Pulmonary doctor, which was the sleep doctor, said Iyonia had Narcolepsy. I had asked what Narcolepsy was and he told me. I had never heard of that before. The doctor started trying Iyonia on different types of medication. Some of the medication did not work on her. He went through so many types of medicines and said that her case was one of the worst cases he had ever dealt with.

Narcolepsy is a chronic sleep disorder characterized by overwhelming daytime drowsiness and sudden attacks of sleep. Iyonia has a hard time staying awake for a long period of time. One day, she had fallen to the ground and started shaking like she was having a seizure. I called the ambulance because I didn't know what was going on. I thought she was having a seizure. The doctor called it something. I called her doctor the next day, and he told me to bring her back in. The doctor said that my daughter also has Cataplexy. Cataplexy is a sudden loss of muscle tone while a person is awake, and it leads to weakness and a loss of voluntary muscle control. It is triggered by sudden, strong emotions such as laughter, fear, anger, stress, or excitement.

One day, my children, mom, and I had gone to my baby brother's graduation. Iyonia started laughing and fell to the ground. People were asking if she was okay. I told them, "Yes." The doctor said not to mess with her, let her come out of her episode on her own. She has been dealing with Narcolepsy with Cataplexy for nine years now. It is a disorder that she will have to live with. I want my daughter driving, but I am nervous that she will fall asleep; but I know I have to trust God and let her go. I bought her first car. Lord knows if anything happens to my daughter, I would go crazy.

My daughter is a Senior in High School. She will be graduating May of this year 2021. She is in NJROTC. She has been in it since 9th grade. She has gotten accepted into Holmes Community

College, Northwest Community College, Itawamba Community College, and Ole Miss University. She said she wanted to major in Psychology. I am proud her. I encourage her to go to college because she has a chance, and she has nothing holding her back from going off to college, living in a dorm, and getting away from Grenada, MS.

MY PAIN IS MY POWER

I became a teen mom again at the age of 17. I remember my Junior year in High School. My water broke. I thought I was just leaking. I told my teacher and asked her for a pad. She sent me to the office. I was given a pad. I went to the bathroom. I put the pad on and went back to class. I was soak and wet. I told my teacher. She told me that my water had broken. I called my mom. She and her husband came and got me and took me to the hospital.

I didn't want my son's dad to know that I was getting ready to deliver my baby because I didn't want him in my room. He worked at the hospital and was at work that day when I delivered my baby boy. His dad named him Rodriquez; I gave him the middle name, Malik. His dad didn't sign the birth certificate because he was saying that my son didn't look like him, and he denied my son for a long time.

I was still staying at my aunt's house at the time. My aunt was helping me now raise not one child, but two children. I didn't know how to be a mom to my kids. I didn't have my mom growing up. My aunt didn't teach me how to be a mom. I didn't have that mother figure in my life. My dad had sent me to live with my aunt when I got pregnant at 13 with my daughter. I gave my kids what they wanted. I spoiled them. I wanted to give them what I didn't have. I didn't know that by doing that it would only hurt me in the long run and in the end.

My children were so used to me buying things for them. They thought they were supposed to get anything that they wanted. I didn't know how to say "NO!" I had never spoken my mind or said no to people as a child. My son was also spoiled. I bought and gave him things, as well as my other child. I felt like I was being a mom to my kids the best way I knew how.

I didn't have anyone to teach me how to be a mom or to discipline my children. I discipline my children the way I thought and knew how they should have been disciplined. As my son got older and started going to school, the teachers had started having problems out of him not listening, talking back, and being disrespectful to them. I had to send my son off to Parkwood Behavioral Health because of his behavior. I was having problems out of him, not wanting to listen to me.

One day, I grabbed my son in his chest by his shirt, my son grabbed me back, and we started tussling. My son fought me, and I fell on his bed. He got on top of me and started punching me in my face and hitting me. I wasn't trying to fight my son back. I just was trying to get him to stop fighting and hitting me. I called the police. The police came and talked to him. He was taken to the Detention Center in Greenwood, MS. He said they let him play the video game. He is now 15 years old. He is in the 9th grade and is in football.

I encourage my son to do better and to stop hanging with the wrong crowd. I love my son. I want nothing but the best for him.

Khloe is my 3rd child and is 3 years old. I love her so much. I don't treat my children any differently from the other. I had Khloe when I was 29 years old. Reality didn't kick in for me until I was 30 years old that I had three children and that I was actually a mother, I was lost.

Khloe too is spoiled. I have a chance to be a better mom and raise her differently than being a teenage mom with my other two children and knowing nothing about raising children. She is shy around other people. She is taking dance classes. I get to see things that Khloe is going to grow up doing. She loves to come home showing me her dances that she learned at dance school. She loves her sister and brother so much.

MY PAIN IS MY POWER

The devil started playing tricks with my mind. I had dark clouds to come over me. I started getting angry, taking things out on my kids and my boyfriend for no reason. The devil had me thinking I was going crazy. I reached out to my pastor and his wife to ask them to pray for me and to ask them what was going on with me. They told me that the enemy doesn't like when you are working on changing your life and getting closer to God, but to keep praying and talking to God.

I remember being at my hotel in Memphis, TN. I had to take my Real Estate exam that next morning. As I laid in the hotel bed, I started dozing off. The devil had me thinking somebody was knocking at my door. The enemy started getting in the bed with me pulling at my sheets.

Then, as I tossed and turned and drifted off, the enemy held me down to the bed. I couldn't talk. I was trying to say the word "Jesus." It then released me!

My favorite scripture in the Bible is "I can do all things through Christ Jesus who strengthens me," Philippians 4:13. My life changed when I was set free, delivered, and healed on September 4, 2020. I have been doing things that I would have never done. I got up in church and gave my testimony on December 13, 2020. I thought I was going to be nervous and scared, but I wasn't. Let me tell you, it's all in the mind! You can do all things through Christ who strengthens you.

I am moving forward with my life and becoming the woman God called me to be and not the person those men instilled in me. There is hope and a God. Trust and believe. I pray my book helps someone. I am passionate about helping others and talking. The enemy wants me to keep quiet about the things that happened to me as a child and up until my adulthood, but I will never hush. I will forever speak my truth and share my story.

I am speaking tonight on "Never Give Up" radio talk show, tonight at 6:30 p.m. central time on March 30, 2021, and sharing my story. I will be speaking on Child Abuse Prevention speaker series on April 8, 2021, and sharing my story. Every time I share my story, I am healing. I not only want to share my story to help myself, but I want to share my story to help others who are going through what I went through or are still going through what I went through.

I want to help stop child rape, child sexual assault, domestic violence, families that attack, neglect, and help people break their silence and speak because their voice matters and needs to be heard.

I am looking to start my own organization and start my own podcast. I am going to help others like myself. I didn't let the backlash stop me from being who God called me to me and the work in His ministry.

Your voice matters and needs to be heard! Too many people are not speaking because of being judged and the fear that has been instilled in them. I pray my book helps you. Remember, speak up and speak out even when your voice trimmers! I am a Domestic Violence Advocate and an Incest Advocate.

Forgiveness Is Everything

23

God came to me in a dream and told me that in order for him to forgive me, I had to forgive myself and forgive everyone who done wrong to me. One time, I was at a point in my life where I found it hard to forgive the first man who raped me and the other four men who manipulated me and took advantage of me. God said for me to let go all of my worries and problems and put them in his hand. I still found it hard to do. I just kept praying.

I finally forgave all five men. I forgave my cousins who had sex with me and who manipulated me into having sex with them. I forgave my aunt for not protecting me. I forgave my dad for sending me to live with my aunt when I got pregnant at the age of 13. I finally had a talk with my dad, and he told me that he only sent me to live with my aunt because he wanted me to be with my family. My dad didn't know his mother or his siblings, so he said he wanted me to grow up around my siblings. I respect and understand that. I forgave my mom for neglecting me and not taking care of me. My mom was 16 years old when she had me. She was just a child herself.

I don't blame my mom, my aunt, or dad. I blame all five of those grown men who knew better than to manipulate a child to have sex with them. Like I said, I was 5 or 6 when I was raped, and the abuse kept happening. Forgiveness is Everything, because if you don't forgive, you can't heal properly and move forward.

I Have Always Wanted To Be A Speaker

24

I have always wanted to be a speaker, and I am now speaking. I first started speaking last year, July 3, 2020, on NASSCA. NASSCA stands for National Association Adult Survivors off Child Abuse. I didn't know I would be opening a door for backlash from my family members and getting attacked by some of them. I felt a relief off of me when I spoke.

I wanted to speak more and share my story. I then spoke on "Your Voices of Hope" podcast on July 13, 2020. I then spoke on "Re-Discover Me" and "Against All Oddz" podcast on October 28, 2020. I spoke again on November 20, 2020, on "Ask a Sex Abuse Survivor." I spoke again on March 22, 2021, on "So LUX Life." I am speaking tonight on Never Give up on March 30, 2021. I will be speaking on April 8, 2021, on

"Child Abuse Prevention" as a speaker.

I look to keep speaking and sharing my story. I am looking to start my own Podcast. I have started a blog called "Being Tanisha." God has delivered me from my pain and past. He is healing me and allowing me to move forward with my life. I never know who I would have been if I wasn't raped and manipulated or went through so much pain and trauma. All I can do is move forward with my life and be the Tanisha today and in the future.

If you would like to hear more about my testimony, I can be found online at:

www.facebookcom/TanishaBankston

Made in the USA
Columbia, SC
08 July 2021

41459052R00072